Inspired Living - Faith-Filled Reflections For A Life Without Limitations
Written by Anita Sechesky

Copyright© 2018 by LWL PUBLISHING HOUSE
A division of Anita Sechesky - Living Without Limitations Inc.

All rights reserved. No part of this publication may be reproduced, distributed or transmitted in any form or by any means, including photocopying, recording, or other electronic or mechanical methods without prior written permission of the publisher, except in the case of brief quotations embodied in critical reviews and certain other noncommercial uses permitted by copyright law. For permission requests, write to the publisher, addressed "Attention: Permissions Coordinator," at the address below.

Publisher's Note: This book is a collection of thoughts and perceptions written at the discretion of the author. LWL PUBLISHING HOUSE uses American English spelling as its standard. Each word usage and sentence structure have remained unaltered as much as possible to retain the authenticity of the visionary's voice.

Anita Sechesky- Living Without Limitations Inc.
Email: lwlclienthelp@gmail.com
Website: www.lwlpublishinghouse.com

Book Layout© 2018 LWL PUBLISHING HOUSE

Inspired Living - Faith-Filled Reflections For A Life Without Limitations
Anita Sechesky - Living Without Limitations Inc.

ISBN 978-1-988867-09-0
ASIN 1988867090

Book Cover: LWL PUBLISHING HOUSE Multimedia Team
Inside Layout: LWL PUBLISHING HOUSE Multimedia Team

Legal Disclaimer	1
Dedication	2
In Gratitude	3
Introduction	4
The Art of Forgiveness	5
Peace is Personal	7
Inspired Living Pages	14 to 33
Prayer of Forgiveness	34
Peace is Perfected	35
Inspired Living Pages	38 to 52
Peace is Powerful	53
Prayer for Peace	59
Inspired Living Pages	60 to 77
Prayer for Healing	78
Grief's Healing Journey	79
About the Author	93

LEGAL DISCLAIMER

The information and content contained within this book Inspired Living - Faith-Filled Reflections For A Life Without Limitations does not substitute any form of professional counsel such as a Psychologist, Physician, Pastor/Minister, Life Coach, or Counselor. The contents and information provided does not constitute professional or legal advice in any way, shape or form.

All written material is a reflection of the author's vision, faith, and insight, based on her personal life and professional experiences, at her discretion. Anita Sechesky – Living Without Limitations Inc. or LWL PUBLISHING HOUSE is not liable or responsible for any of the specific details, descriptions of people, places or things, personal interpretations, stories and experiences contained within. The Publisher is not liable for any misrepresentations, false or unknown statements, actions, or judgments made by any of the contributors or their chapter contents in this book. Each contributor is responsible for their own submissions and has shared their stories in good faith to encourage others.

Any decisions you make and the outcomes thereof are entirely your own doing. Under no circumstances can you hold the author, LWL PUBLISHING HOUSE, or "Anita Sechesky – Living Without Limitations Inc." liable for any actions that you take. You agree not to hold the author, LWL PUBLISHING HOUSE, or "Anita Sechesky – Living Without Limitations Inc." liable for any loss or expense incurred by you, as a result of materials, advice, coaching or mentoring offered within.

The information offered in this book is intended to be general information with respect to general life issues. Information is offered in good faith; however, you are under no obligation to use this information.

Nothing contained in this book shall be considered legal, financial, or actuarial advice.

It may introduce what a Professional Life Coach, Counselor, Pastor/Minister or Therapist may discuss with you at any given time during personal sessions. The advice contained herein is not meant to replace the Professional roles of a physician or any of the above-mentioned professions.

Dedication

It is a blessing to dedicate this beautiful book to both of my parents, Jean & Jetty Seergobin.

I can honestly say with all of my heart that my personal values, faith, and appreciation for others comes from their loving example.

Thank you Mom & Dad

Love, Your Daughter

Anita

In Gratitude

Special Thanks of Gratitude to God, my Heavenly Father.
It is because of you that I can do all things.
May it always be pleasing to you.

My children, Nathaniel & Sammy - You are my Joy and blessings. Everything I do is for both of you.
My husband, Stephen - Thank you for your loving support and dedication to see this project to completion.
My Mom & Dad - I am grateful for your unfailing love, support and guidance.
My Mom-in-Law - I'm so blessed to have you in my life.

LWL Media Support Team - You are the best! Thank you for your patience in perfecting this beautiful book.

A extra special thanks to all my former patients, nursing colleagues, clients, family & friends - Each of you have inspired the energy and consideration of this project.

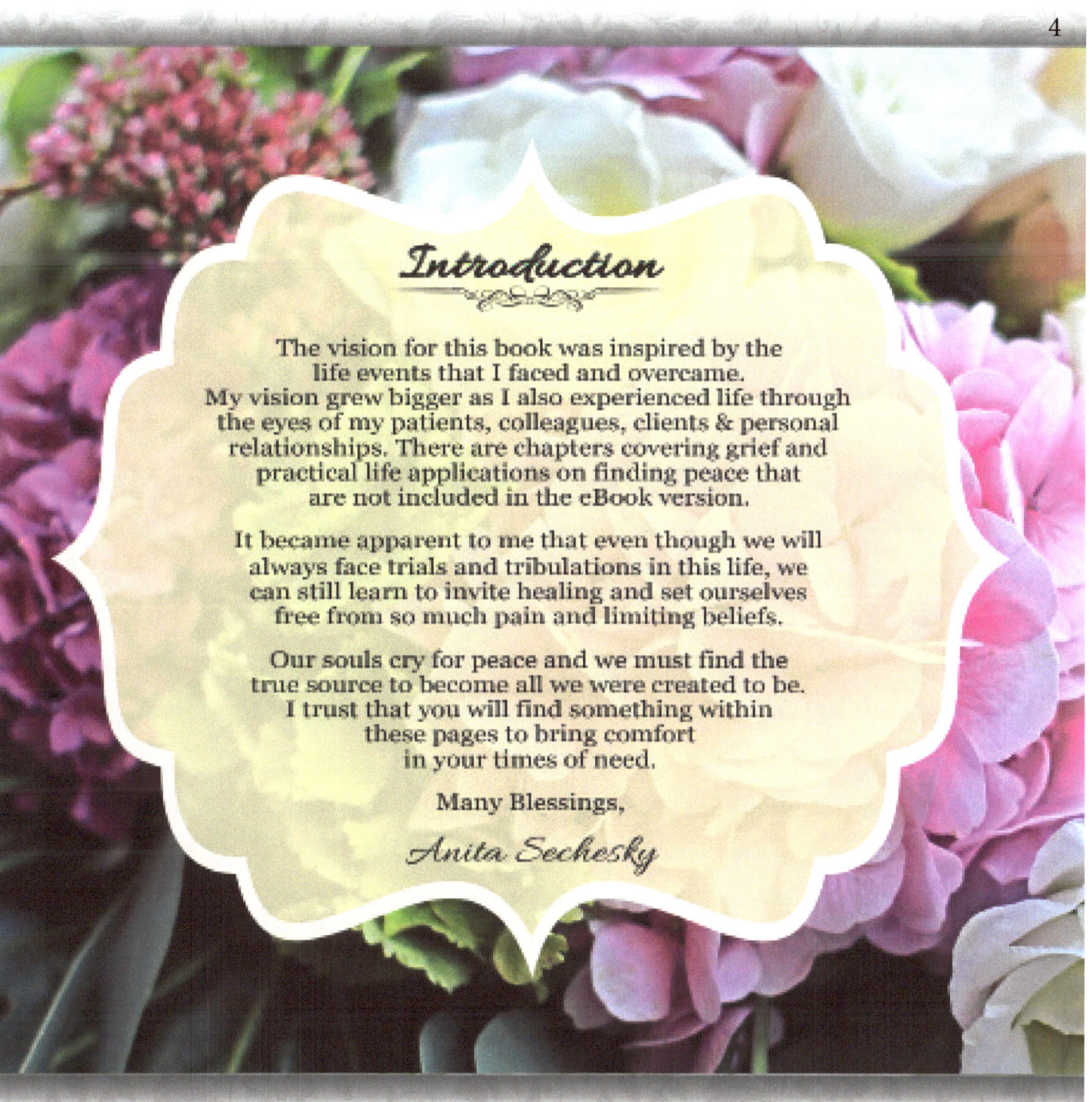

Introduction

The vision for this book was inspired by the life events that I faced and overcame.
My vision grew bigger as I also experienced life through the eyes of my patients, colleagues, clients & personal relationships. There are chapters covering grief and practical life applications on finding peace that are not included in the eBook version.

It became apparent to me that even though we will always face trials and tribulations in this life, we can still learn to invite healing and set ourselves free from so much pain and limiting beliefs.

Our souls cry for peace and we must find the true source to become all we were created to be. I trust that you will find something within these pages to bring comfort in your times of need.

Many Blessings,

Anita Sechesky

The Art of Forgiveness

Dear Friend:

Some BAD words were spoken over your life at some point that you're either aware of or not. It's time to CANCEL those words and their effects now. God's love brings restoration.

Consider adapting "The Art of Forgiveness" into your self-care routine. This can easily be done by reflecting on events that resulted in unpleasant or unresolved feelings which become your limitations. As a result, your life choices, attitudes, relationships, and even health may be adversely affected by those heavy emotions you let fester for too long. It may even show up as stress or anxiety, leading to more serious health conditions if you are not healed emotionally, spiritually, and mentally.

Once you put yourself first, you can easily make conscious decisions to understand and accept where forgiveness is needed in all relationships as you cannot change the people, circumstances, or events from the past. You can only change how you perceive things. Begin to write down the names that come to your mind. It doesn't matter how far back you go as you envision those experiences, and say to your offenders, *"I forgive..." "I now release myself from all destructive soul ties, abuse, pain, rejection, and disappointments you have caused me, knowingly or unknowingly."*

I encourage you to reflect on your feelings. Choose to see your offenders asserting themselves and understand they are victims of their own circumstances. Give yourself permission to be the mature and confident person who is capable of changing your perception of past memories.

Once you have done this with the entire list, you may experience feelings of emotional release over a period of time as those bondages no longer have control over you, unless you allow it. Even though words have power, negative cycles can be replaced with positive emotional reinforcement.

Now that you have completed this process, recognize that God gave you the freedom of choices to make a difference in your life regardless of how others behave.

Remove your daily limitations by always choosing Forgiveness.

Anita Sechesky.

Peace is Personal

In order for an individual to acquire a true nature of peace for self – from a heart of love and gratitude, there must be a divine connection to our source, whatever we may perceive that to be. We all come from somewhere outside of who we are in our physical state of being. For some people, this means a divine connection to our Creator and God of the universe. Eventually, we must strive to understand that no matter what we are going through, our lives are still connected so that what we feel, think, or perceive may be affected by our actions and attitudes towards any given situation at any moment.

We must positively develop into people who choose to understand and appreciate one another. As we journey inside our hearts and souls, we discover a desire pulling us into a mindful state of constant gratitude, safety, and happiness. We might still find ourselves in moments of unpleasant emotions disrupting our inner calmness and security. It's not an easy journey as many will admit because there will be times of confusion and unbalance. As confident as we appear, we can still become our worst critic and many times the limitations and perceptions that we hold on to are based upon the most unique, disturbing experiences affecting us during times of weakness and vulnerability.

As individuals conditioned to react and respond, our behaviors are based on the things that we are constantly exposed to. They say habits are easily formed by the unconscious and selective process of who we are choosing to be associated with. Many times, if we don't pay attention to these choices, we mirror the behaviors and actions of the very people we despise. It's not always easy to separate

ourselves from individuals we have gotten comfortable being around, regardless of the nature of the connection. Because of this, many will continue to stay in damaging relationships, refusing to step outside of their associations. When this happens, we are left in a stagnated growth emotionally and mentally, all the while life keeps on going. We continue to age and mature as our appearance changes, but our emotional well-being is slowly destroyed. Sadly, we allow so many of our life decisions to fall into a familiar pattern of perceived safety. As a result, any potential within us is deeply scarred and languishing because we have not allowed ourselves the proper amount of introspective observation to gain peace, process the experience, and find solitude with those painful situations. We become limited in our lives. The peace that should be there to bring in the confidence and well-being is constantly overshadowed and cannot shine into the greatest light it can possibly become.

In order for there to be permanent change and recognizable healing, we must confidently choose the "Act of Forgiveness" as the positive channel to release all of our negative and pent up emotions that can eventually decay the inside of us. By allowing these new and positive thoughts to flow into our hurt emotions, we are consciously shifting the energy around us to attract more peace and gratitude. You see, unforgiveness, anger, hate, and all their negative behaviors are of low vibration and cannot produce anything good as a

result. Sadly, this is still misunderstood and many people are not aware of why they may have a false sense of peaceful tranquility. If one strives for a healthy and confident mindset, all negative attitudes

and behaviors must be addressed and determined by what kind of attachments have actually been permitted into one's life. So many times, we will see individuals who attest to having the ultimate achievement we all desire, that of inner harmony and satisfaction, magnified by the power of love, financial security, and social contentment. They want us to believe they've arrived. It's up to us to determine what we see and what they want us to see. Every single person must interact and grow from relationships with others. There's just no way we can avoid this human experience. As we become more connected with those outside our inner circle, we then start to examine ourselves differently, as every connection brings its own set of experiences, for example, more setbacks, failures, challenges, disappointments, and opportunities to grow and develop into our best self yet. Whatever the event, life will always present us many chances to change our responses. The choice to be at peace, despite everything, is always ours to make.

When we come to understand that being centered is when the heart is at peace, our divine connection to God of our universe becomes a confidence that is unwavering and reassures us in times of uncertainty that we can get through just about anything if we believe in ourselves and something bigger than we can conceive. For someone to achieve this state of gratitude, they must understand that life is a story that they get to co-create. Our emotional state is created by our reality, based on our attachment to the outcome, so when seeking a peaceful experience in life, we must comprehend that there is a requirement of us to also put effort into developing the miracle of peace, through mediation, forgiveness, prayer or acceptance of a situation.

Often, we find ourselves in events where we cannot get into a meditative or calming state and there is so much happening around us, we simply cannot achieve the balance and stability we need to not be personally affected by our environment. It's at these moments that a trained mind will follow the rules of grounding ourselves into a place of security. We can do this through visualization and prayer or a positive affirmation will work just as well. Most people choose to associate miracles and positive outcomes to the understanding that they have deposited a portion of faith, moral thoughts, and optimistic attitudes towards their anticipated outcome. Many times, life's painful experiences are the contributing factors causing people to demand within themselves that which makes them invincible.

Throughout life's journey, the human spirit perseveres through many difficulties that would have otherwise taken us down had we not had an ounce of faith coupled with peace that prevails. As we are pulled in many directions, we establish patterns of emotional perceptions based on many factors. This book reflects on these such things of great magnitude. For instance, developing and seeking a life of peace and gratitude commences in early childhood and is most often influenced by the content we are exposed to from other human behaviours regardless of who they are and where they fit into our lives, both negative and positive. It will impact the very essence of that person who experiences these situations to determine what level of peace they have in their lives at that moment and do they want to maintain it regardless of whatever it takes. These experiences may include the loss of a loved one, having to face life-threatening conditions, a devastating diagnosis, traumatic and abusive

relationships, family rifts, as well as other moments not fondly recalled. As we choose to remember, many times what happens may not be directly associated to who we are, but life will always give us experiences aligned to the vibrational energy of those we are closely connected with. Once we keep in mind that we might even be a receiver from the energies of those we are not even associated with any longer, the very nature that we have interacted with someone at any given point, vibrationally sets us up for some kind of universal reminder of that person. That's why we must diligently strive to develop a peaceful oasis that imamates from within, as responsible beings come to recognize and appreciate how magnificent a gift it really is to rediscover our confidence in our peaceful mindset and emotional intelligence is the reason we have the ability to gain this ownership of our lives despite what circumstances we face in our daily lives.

By understanding that our lives have equal value, just as those we are connected with, allows our higher selves to appreciate and connect with others on a more authentic and sincere level. This is a huge deal for those who have suffered from neglect or abusive and traumatic experiences where they were vulnerable enough to allow the situation to hurt them deeply. Although this may have happened unexpectedly, it does not mean it was the victim's fault in any way, shape, or form. It just means that the awareness of the pain has actually strengthened the individual enough to shift them from a victim mentality to self-empowerment and strong enough to maintain a level of peace and healings through various steps possibly involving forgiveness, not only of the individual who inflicted the wrong, but an acceptance to forgive one's self

for being in the situation to begin with.

A heart of peace and gratitude is beautifully cultured from deep reflective and often times the most life-altering experiences. People will carry on doing the same things repetitively, supposing a changed outcome each time, and still not have the peace they are seeking after. Regrettably, they don't identify that the resolution is familiarizing themselves to a whole new perspective that unlocks windows of opportunities, allowing them the ability to heal, evolve and effortlessly grow. I often wonder about how it would impact the lives of those who feel trapped and isolated, that nothing is impossible if they choose to be understanding and abundance mindset to appreciate that in order to love the life they have been blessed with, they must develop a continual process of forgiveness and love allowing the peace to be recognized in their interactions with others in their lives. Releasing the baggage and sadness resulting from the unforgiveness and pain will allow the stagnant negative energy and low vibrations to be released from their energetic physiology. As they choose to make an effort in their thought processes, emotional intelligence, verbal and emotional triggers, as well as the behavioral reactions towards everyone around them, the vibrations remain positive and higher positive energy from the power of love envelopes the peaceful aura around and through them creating a simple but significant change in thoughts, actions and external attitudes. Once we choose to continue attracting more positive and peaceful experiences and it will begin healing our very souls.

Examining my own life, I have also experienced the struggle to hold my peace when I had no control over the outcome based on actions of the other individual

 involved. I learned that if there are unsettled events in my life, there will always directly be some sort of disruption and blockage of peaceful blessings and gratitude. This is what permits a renewal of perspectives to create a life shift in future viewpoints and it's results.

Peace is personal, but it still recognizes that it is contingent on the interactions of all people we are connected with. However, it is one of the most satisfying voyages we can all step into. May your journeys be peaceful.

Sharing is the essence of caring & prosperity always finds me because I have an abundance mindset.

—Anita Sechesky

Your hands hold the healing for the lives still within your reach, but your heart's outreach can be even greater.

—Anita Sechesky

*You are
creating
the world
around you
by the beauty
in your words.*

~Anita Sechesky

Humanity is an extension of who you are. Choose to accept and believe in everyone, not just your own.

-Anita Sechesky

Life is more precious when you see your humanity reflected in everyone.

~ Anita Sechesky

Everything in my life is a blessing: the good, the bad & the yucky because I get to choose how it will benefit me.

~Anita Sechesky

Choose to celebrate the person you are becoming each new day by taking better care of yourself.

~ Anita Sechesky

*I choose to
speak life into
my body by
every prayer
that I bless
my food
and drink with.*

-Anita Sechesky

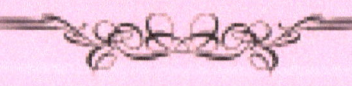

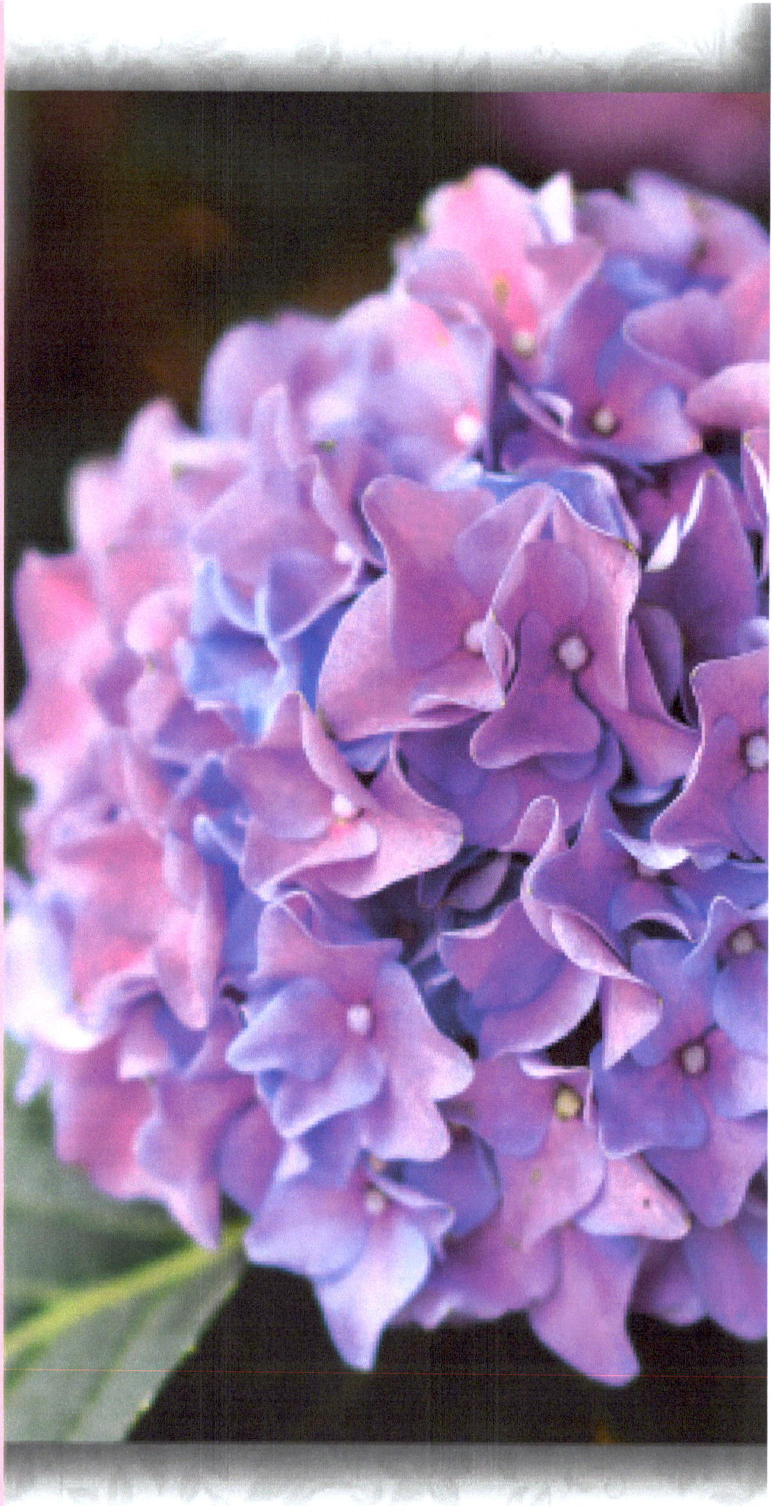

When you see the children of this generation, send a prayer their way for the future is in their hands.

— Anita Sechesky

Abundance is my birthright as a child of God. I accept every blessing that has my name on it.

—Anita Sechesky

"Trust in the LORD with all your heart and lean not on your own understanding. In all your ways acknowledge Him and He will direct your path."

~ Proverbs 3:5-6 NIV

Living your life without limitations begins the moment you choose to forgive and release without regrets.

~Anita Sechesky

Your beautiful smile is the essence of your soul energetically illuminating everyone it touches.

-Anita Sechesky

Beauty does not stop on the surface of your skin. It reaches beyond the dimensions of your soul.

~Anita Sechesky

Unconditional love begins with you. If you want love, you must be Love in action.

~Anita Sechesky

Peace is Perfected

What are the many ways that you have witnessed or experienced the most beautiful or perfect feeling of peace and tranquility? Did it take having to step away from the busy commotions of life to re-discover the beauty in the world around you? Or did you create a peaceful oasis in your own home and natural surroundings, with little things like candles, incense, or moments of relaxation?

My reason for including this within this beautiful book is that I've come to understand that peace is something we are always going to look to perfect whether we realize it or not. Once you have had a taste of something that envelops your very soul to that of total bliss and happiness, why wouldn't you choose to have more? We are all connected and with that conscious awareness, we can come to a greater appreciation of attaining this added value to our lives. We constantly long for this fulfilling desire to quench our souls into the luxury and necessity of personal and peaceful perfection.

Although luxurious self-care is something that's not freely available to everyone, we can still achieve simple and healing opportunities as we go about our daily lives in a world that is constantly changing. Social media has made it seem that the world is in our backyard, therefore when others are affected by events or circumstances, we begin to feel this overwhelming burden also. We are prompted to conjure emotional responses based on the fact that we are empathetic beings with greater outreach through our connections, so we always share life experiences and memories with others regardless of the situation. This is when a person begins to understand how valuable their

small acts of peace and kindness are towards others, as it creates a perfect balance in our own environment and ultimately becomes a heart-warming experience for everyone else we are associated with.

I believe that in order for peace to be perfected in our lives, one must truly learn to love themselves and those close to them in order to appreciate anyone outside their immediate circle without hesitancy. Otherwise, how could anyone honestly live at peace with those whom they have no natural connection? The true power in loving yourself opens up the reality that we are choosing to accept all of our imperfections. As we willingly choose to think this way, it becomes easier to accept everyone as well, imperfections and all. Keep in mind, this also requires you to let go of everything that does not serve your greatest self any longer. Choosing to love your inner circle connections or those who know and appreciate you sets your loving peace apart for that of our outside world. If you don't allow others to negatively influence you any longer, you'll always create peace around you everywhere you go. Once you have made your peaceful intentions clear and focused, peace will always find its way back to you. You are a peaceful person and deserve to live a life filled with unlimited peace and abundance. This positive mindset increases the vibrations around you, and positively affects the way that you see yourself, and in turn how others will see you as well.

When you reflect the amount of wasted time and draining energy it takes to create drama

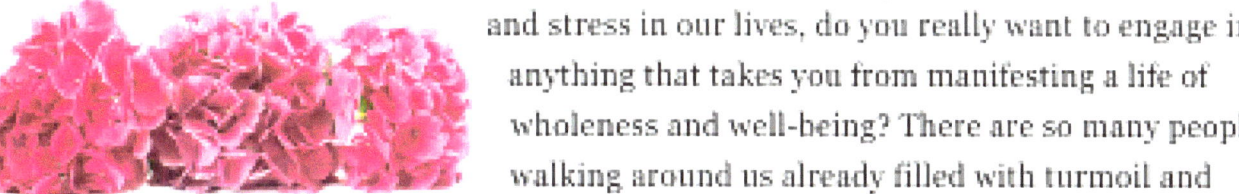

and stress in our lives, do you really want to engage in anything that takes you from manifesting a life of wholeness and well-being? There are so many people walking around us already filled with turmoil and

pain. The stressful baggage they choose to carry every day is not getting any lighter as it just keeps attracting more and more negativity and harm. I believe it takes a person with a big heart to be grateful for the life they have, all the relationships they've been blessed with. Choosing to live in gratitude towards others will always build a better life.

This world is filled with people who possess so much peaceful potential, yet they still feel hopeless and distraught. They no longer have dreams or desires because they are discouraged and demoralized by the traumatic or painful events they keep re-living in their daily lives. This is a testament to why I believe there is so much more remaining for everyone to do when it comes to perfecting the peace in, and around us. If we choose to help others who are hopeless and without peace, find healing for themselves and their loved ones, then we have brought a little piece of heaven to earth.

Thankfully, I've had the privilege to provide nursing care to people from various regions around the world, allowing my eyes to be opened to what is actually happening to so many others in my own neighborhood. My experiences often left me feeling distressed; they are just like everyone else needing to be loved and accepted to heal. People need a peaceful environment to thrive and live fulfilled lives, regardless of where they are on this planet. I choose to see value in everyone equally. What an amazing world full of precious souls we have yet to reach, one life, one voice, one song that is perfected by the resounding beauty of peace that is felt throughout all the ages, nations, and races. Let's help create peace in every corner of the globe and apply liberally with love, empathy, and grace. Peace is perfected through one life, one interaction at a time.

You are not the limitations that people place on you. You are exactly who you choose to become.

—Anita Sechesky

Surround yourself fully in the light of God's healing grace and unlimited love.

—Anita Sechesky

Miracles are always available for you at the whisper of your heart's cry.

~Anita Sechesky

Love always creates a life worth living and keeps it safe within its arms.

~ Anita Sechesky

You are filled with so much potential. Every opportunity that comes your way is manifested within your soul.

~Anita Sechesky

Friendship is God's way of sending His Love through the earth angels we meet along our journey.

—Anita Sechesky

Good parents are a blessing and their unconditional love is God's way of saying He will never leave us.

~Anita Sechesky

"A cheerful heart is good medicine, but a crushed spirit dries up the bones."

~ Proverbs 17:22 NIV

My heart beats with Hope and it creates new opportunities for me to prosper and praise my Creator.

−Anita Sechesky

My life is a miracle and I choose to see miracles everywhere around me.

—Anita Sechesky

You can turn your mistakes into opportunities to shift your perception and determine new approaches in life.

-Anita Sechesky

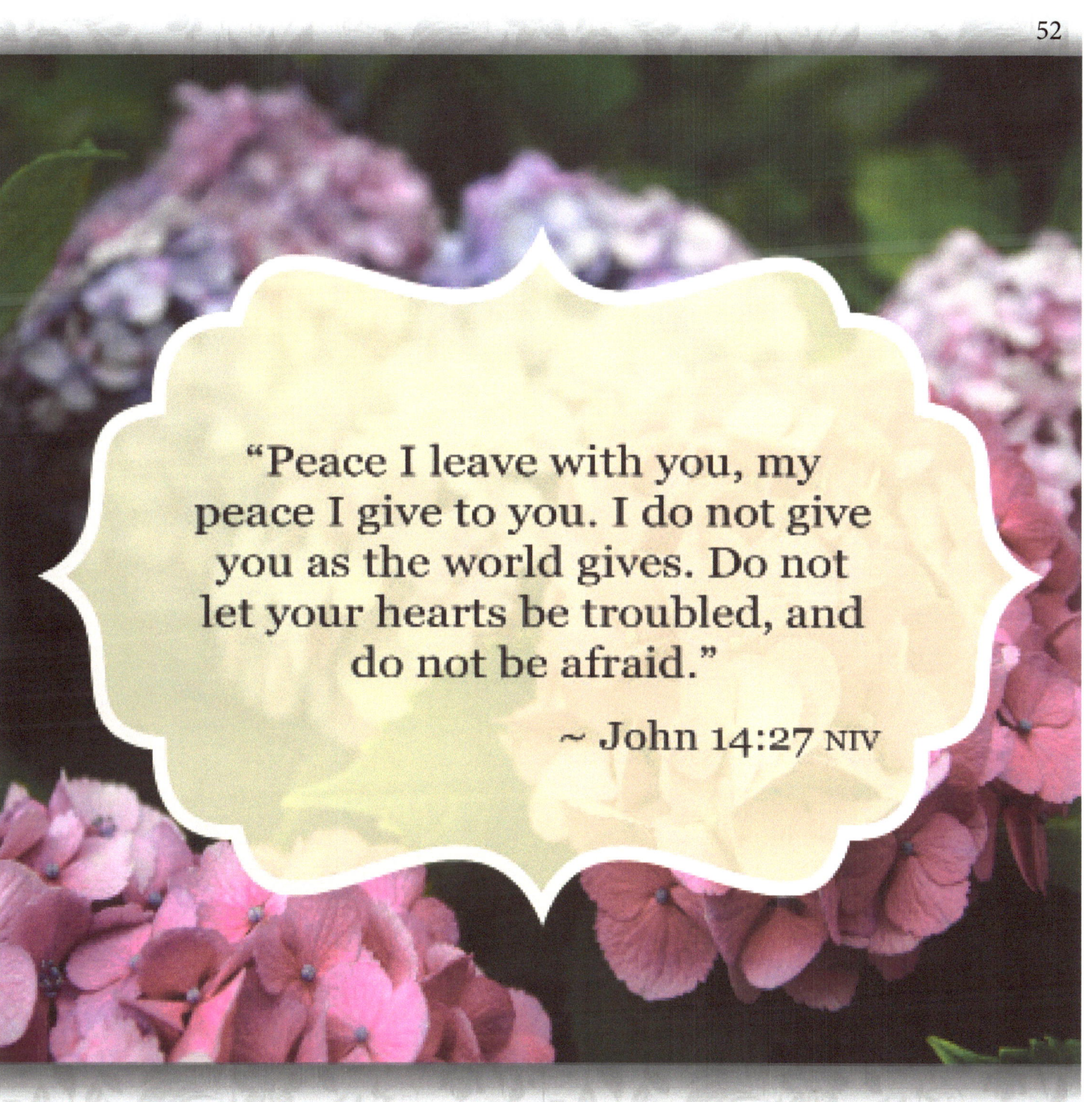

"Peace I leave with you, my peace I give to you. I do not give you as the world gives. Do not let your hearts be troubled, and do not be afraid."

~ John 14:27 NIV

Peace is Powerful

Often times our perspectives of the people in our lives is affected by what's going on inside of us. As sensitive individuals, these relationships play a key role in the way we show up in the world. We identify ourselves, based on the emotional experiences we have lived through, we become a product of our environment. That being said, when we are aware that we cannot change anyone but ourselves, our true peaceful evolution of awareness and enlightenment powerfully evolves. Personal relationships validate our existence, allowing us the freedom to become our very best selves.

Even successful people started somewhere when no one knew who they were, and they probably experienced anxiety, stress, or discouragement. Yet, at the very moment they were going to let it all go, someone offered them kind words of encouragement.

Peace is powerful because it affects every facet of our lives. It's the foundation of how we respond and interact with every person we encounter. It causes us to take responsibility for our behaviors because everyone is affected by the words that come out of our mouths. The actions we display towards others is an indication of our mental health and well-being. For instance, if we don't process our experiences and determine the difference between right and wrong, or what's acceptable in our society, our outward actions and behaviors reveal a disruption in our lives. Therefore, our attitudes are projected onto others and can make a difference between forming a friendship or creating an enemy.

A healthy mindset allows us this opportunity to fully comprehend how to establish a balanced life of peace towards everyone we are associated with. Although life has no guarantees, once we learn the various ways to

create and find peace, we heal our bodies, minds, and spirits. Choosing to live this way will continually attract a peaceful and harmonious lifestyle. We will notice how our health greatly improves, and our focus is determined and intended. The stresses of life quickly dissipate, and we easily recognize the need to be there for others instead of introspectively looking at our own selfish needs. Stepping outside of our comfort zones permits us the power to help others find their own healing, hope, and peace in their lives also. Developing a habit of peace and gratitude consistently attracts good things into our lives, there is only added joy in living this way. Relationships that were once strained begin to heal and take on new possibilities, allowing for more like-minded individuals to be welcomed into our lives.

I encourage you to seriously examine all your relationships within your inner and outer circle. As a Registered Nurse, I have personally observed how traumatic it can be when family members lose their loved ones due to health issues. It's especially disturbing when there are gaps in the communication process and the unhealthy aspects of the relationship prevents individuals from visiting their loved ones during the end of life stage. Many times, I have seen so many precious souls leave this world with broken hearts and spirits because of family disputes and disagreements that were never addressed years ago. It's a sad thing to witness the look in their eyes, worried if their loved ones will come to visit with them before their earthly departure. Our lives have no guarantees, but we can make the choices to love and place value where it belongs in the healing of those closest to us and give ourselves the blessing to also experience spiritual release and healing that is filled with divine peace and comfort. Once life is over, there are no second chances. Make peace before it's too late.

My body is meticulously designed to create health and restoration when I treat it with gentle loving care and attention.

~Anita Sechesky

People will always need your inspiration. Never let an opportunity to be genuine pass you by.

-Anita Sechesky

Reflect on your journey but don't stay there. Life is filled with so much hope and potential ready to come your way.

—Anita Sechesky

When I choose
to see the
healing power
of love,
I can easily
release all
harmful thoughts
that serve me
no good.

—Anita Sechesky

Prayer for Peace

Dearest Heavenly Father;

As your child, I come to you because you are a very present help in trouble. Please give me the peace that passeth all understanding and grace to overcome all anxieties and challenges I am going through right now.

Amen.

> *It's my life to choose every thought of peace, hope, love & happiness. I am that Powerful!*
>
> ~Anita Sechesky

The rain is the blessing that all flowers need, our tears are the healing that our souls must release.

-Anita Sechesky

"He heals the brokenhearted and binds up their wounds."

~ Psalm 147:3 NIV

I am grateful for every dollar that comes my way. I choose to joyfully bless others and I gladly receive blessings.

-Anita Sechesky

I love to celebrate the success of others because it cancels jealousy and brings my blessings closer to me.

—Anita Sechesky

Success happens when you empower your mind and see the greatness within yourself.

~ Anita Sechesky

Inspired Living Tip

Choosing to be alone should be a time of refreshing and personal growth.

~Anita Sechesky

You're always
in control of
your emotions.
How you
respond to others
will create
the energy
you live by.

-Anita Sechesky

Grief is a journey that honors the souls who have left us behind. Take all the time you need, but eventually you must continue on your own living destiny.

—Anita Sechesky

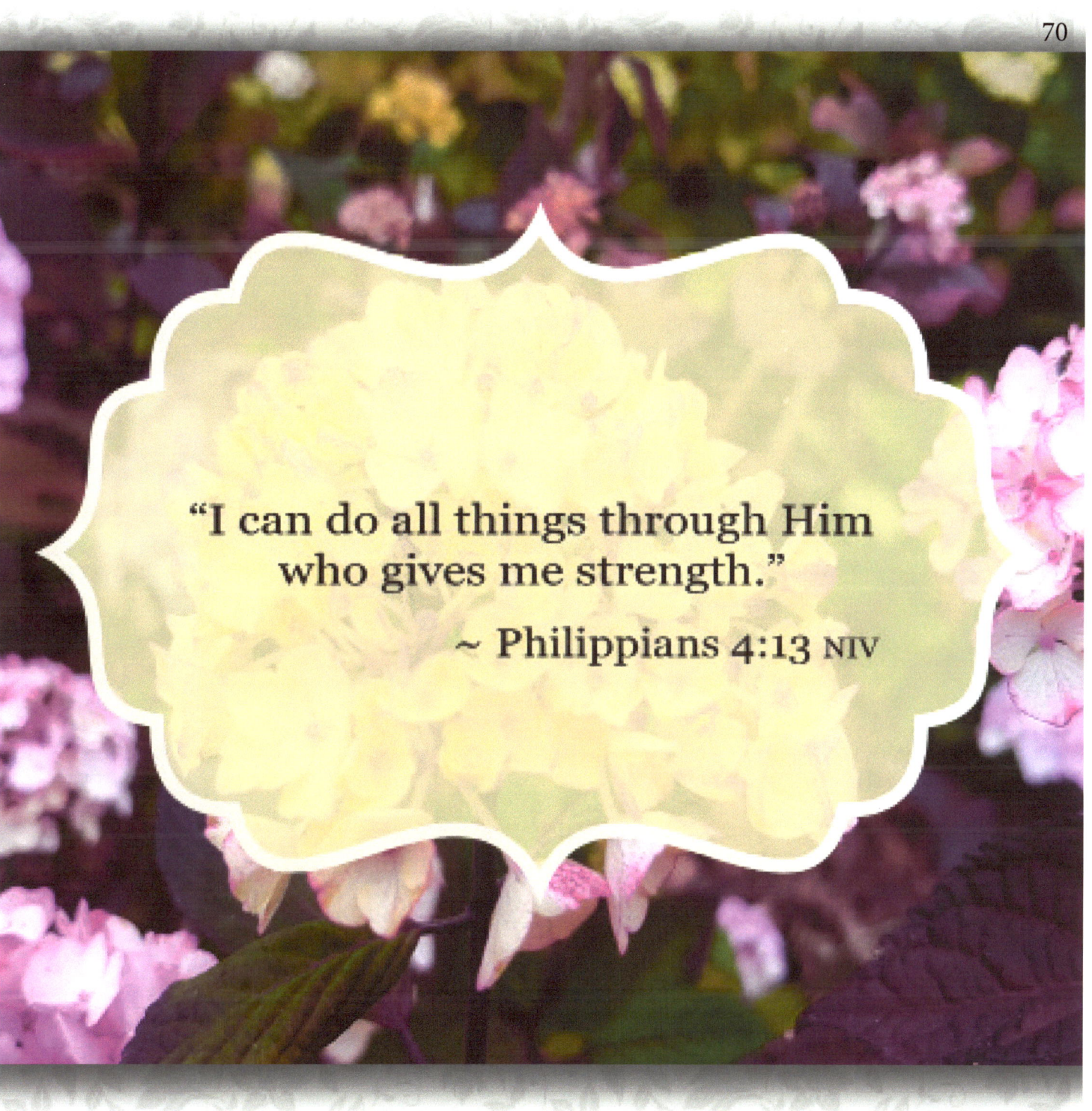

Sunshine is a warm hug from God, our Creator. We can freely step into it's gentle embrace.

— Anita Sechesky

Before I close my eyes at night, I peacefully reflect on all the good things in my life & my sleep restores every cell of my body.

~Anita Sechesky

You are more beautiful than the faithful flowers blooming under the summer sun.

~Anita Sechesky

> *I freely let go and cancel all negative, destructive, & hurtful words spoken over my life and everything that concerns my well-being.*
>
> ~ Anita Sechesky

Grief's Healing Jouney

Inspired Living can mean something different for everyone. Often, it's the birth of a child that gives us hope for our future filled with so much joy. But the strongest influence for me in my life occurred after the loss of my first child. My beautiful daughter, Jasmine Rose, was born sleeping (as it is so lovingly referred to now) on December 19th, 1998 – just two days shy of my own birthday on December 21st.

My pregnancy was perfect, and my doctor appointments were great with good reports every month. Around this time, the internet was quickly gaining popularity, so my husband and I signed up for a month-by-month virtual pregnancy guide that provided much insight for new parents-to-be with beautiful three-dimensional animations of how our baby was growing and developing daily. You can only imagine the excitement on our daily check-ins.

It wasn't until two weeks before baby Jasmine's due date and during my final monthly OBGYN appointment that I found myself asking my Obstetrician to please induce me because I felt it was time for Jasmine to be born. My request was quickly denied because it was a first pregnancy and uneventful, so there were no concerns medically. My husband and I then went into the ultrasound room to have our baby recorded in Utero. The technician decided to answer a personal phone call, which turned into an extended conversation, while still recording with the ultrasound camera. As new parents-to-be, we never thought anything of it and assumed he knew his job and was proficient as he appeared to be so skilled.

After our appointment, we happily drove back three hours to our small community in Northern Ontario with the video tape of our baby. It was the middle of winter with minus 40-degree temperatures, so we didn't want to be on the highway after the sunset, which occurs very early in the north. I think back to so many emotions that were flooding me in that bitter cold winter of 1998. But I will never forget the deepest most devastating feelings of being rejected a dozen times going to my community emergency room and being turned away by the nurses on shift. The responses I often heard were "Everything is fine," "The heartbeat drops during the pregnancy," "It's your first and sometimes you can worry too much." I even recall a friend of ours telling us in the hospital parking to not give up with whatever we were going through because his wife and him were also turned away and ended up having a miscarriage.

When I share this experience about the loss of my daughter, please keep in mind that it took me over ten years to openly discuss it without becoming emotional. My years of processing involved seeking counsel from support groups that only left me feeling more depressed because the facilitators could not connect emotionally with me or the other group members, going to many different church services for spiritual guidance, calling prayer support hot lines, reading tons of self-help books, and going through PTSD (Post Traumatic Stress Disorder). I finally had enough strength to take back control of my emotional healing and found the courage I needed through my personal relationship with God. You see, after the initial loss of our daughter, I couldn't even find the words to pray, so I asked my husband and my mom to be my voice in prayer for me so that God knew I wasn't mad or blaming him. I just didn't know how to talk to God, knowing full well that

my beautiful child was with Him in heaven. Eventually, I reached out and God showed me that He was always there.

My faith has helped me to understand my grief through the capacity of the miracle of life by carrying a child full-term. Then I experienced the trauma of death within my body and had my own near-death experience the night before my scheduled delivery when I was hovering above my body with my daughter's spirit. Next was the releasing of her precious life and all the potential dreams attached to her through the closure of giving birth and then burying her a couple of days later. On the day of the funeral, I witnessed something that made my whole world perspective shift drastically. I observed that all life had value to not only the people we are connected with, but to those who still carry on in the world around us after we die. It was during Jasmine Rose's funeral procession in Thunder Bay, Ontario, my heart softened and shifted profoundly for a community that represented what I had negatively experienced growing up in Northern Ontario until that moment: years of rejection, hate and even racism. I found a new love for the people and respect I never thought I would ever feel. God Bless Thunder Bay, where my sweet baby girl forever sleeps. It will always hold a special place in my heart.

For those who have never experienced the loss of someone close to them, imagine following the Hearst that is carrying your baby and as you are riding behind it, you notice a strange phenomenon that's hard to put into words. For me, it was as if the world had stopped spinning and every single vehicle on both sides of the road pulled over in honor of our little princess. It was the most profound and yet beautiful thing to observe and

even though some people may not understand that because she was born sleeping. Her soft, black hair had baby curls, her beautiful eyelashes were long and curly, her cheeks were soft and chubby, and she had the cutest little dimple chin that I would have kissed all day, like I did with her brothers. Her fingers were long and slender, perfect for playing the piano, and her feet were long and perfect to fit into beautiful shoes like a princess. Her nose was like a little rosebud and her ears were so sweetly shaped. I look at myself in the mirror and still see her forehead and eyebrows. To this day, we have never looked at her video recording because it's too painful to see her smiling and playing when she heard our voices. Life truly is a gift.

The loss of child is an experience that cannot always be put into words because it feels so surreal to speak of a life that wanted to live. She only experienced life from within me and that's where she knew of her daddy and grandparents. She was protected from the harsh, cold world, yet because of uncontrollable circumstances that mommy and daddy tried to intervene in, she lost her dreams and hopes to know the faces, loving arms, and the voices she only heard from within me. I have lived for so many years with the knowledge that my own womb could not keep my baby girl safe, and it was not until some time had gone by did I understand the need to forgive myself for holding onto the guilt and shame that was not mine to own.

I've had no choice but to choose peaceful forgiveness over and over because even though I now have two sons, my heart still remembers the first love of my daughter. Being a mother is something we don't get trained for; its a blessing to carry a child and bring them into the world. It's also a responsibility that changes you forever.

Grief opens many doors of disappointments and can cause us to become unhealthy if we lose our focus on living past our loss. It's not always easy but consider how your loved one would want your life to be after their earthy departure. We would give greater honor to them by actively making little steps in finding our strength to carry on without them day by day.

We can choose to know that they will never be forgotten and that their love for us never died but only transitioned to a powerful eternal loving and healing energy that we can access any given time should we choose to reflect.

We can then turn our moments of heartache into moments of something purposeful when we give back to others as a special way of saying "Because you are on longer here, I choose to help _____ in your memory."

As a nurse, Certified Professional Coach, and someone who experienced grief first-hand, I recognize that varying degrees of anxiety and stress may occur because of personal loss, resulting in a disruption or imbalance of activities of daily living. Therefore, it is very important to stay consistent with regular medical check ups and talk with your doctor about your loss and feelings. Then your doctor can monitor you and recommend further professional support if required for your best interest. However, you should always know that you are ultimately responsible for choosing the best life you want to live by staying healthy, getting regular exercise, fresh air, eating a balance diet, drinking enough water throughout the day, daily prayer and meditation, plus getting a good night's sleep is essential self-care required to heal the mind, body & spirit. Add to this by focusing on the

positive things in our lives, and maintain healthy communication with family, friends, and support systems. That's how setting precious time aside to cope with personal loss is a powerful way of giving our loved ones a special place in our daily lives without feelings of guilt or remorse. Eventually, we may find that life is moving quickly, and we may not have thought of our loved ones in a while. It's okay to accept that as the years go by, we naturally develop new things to do and focus on. But keeping a healthy perspective by planning special days that are dedicated to remembering our loved one is always beautiful. Know that they will always love you and distance does not change pure love. It only remains painful and life-changing for us because we were left behind as they continued their journey for eternity. As a child of God, my hope lies in the promise that one day I will be reunited with my beautiful baby girl forever and ever.

Dear friend; I lift you up in my prayers if you are dealing with loss and the journey of grief is unbearable and still difficult for you right now. Please know that you are not alone and even though others may not understand, hold on to your memories and find strength from within. There is no shame in love, and you have a right to grieve as long as it does not bring harm to you. As lonely as it may feel on some days, you don't have to face it alone. There is always Jesus, God's son, and His heavenly angels that will surround and comfort you...just ask.

In loving memory ~ Jasmine Rose Sechesky
March 1998 - December 19th, 1998

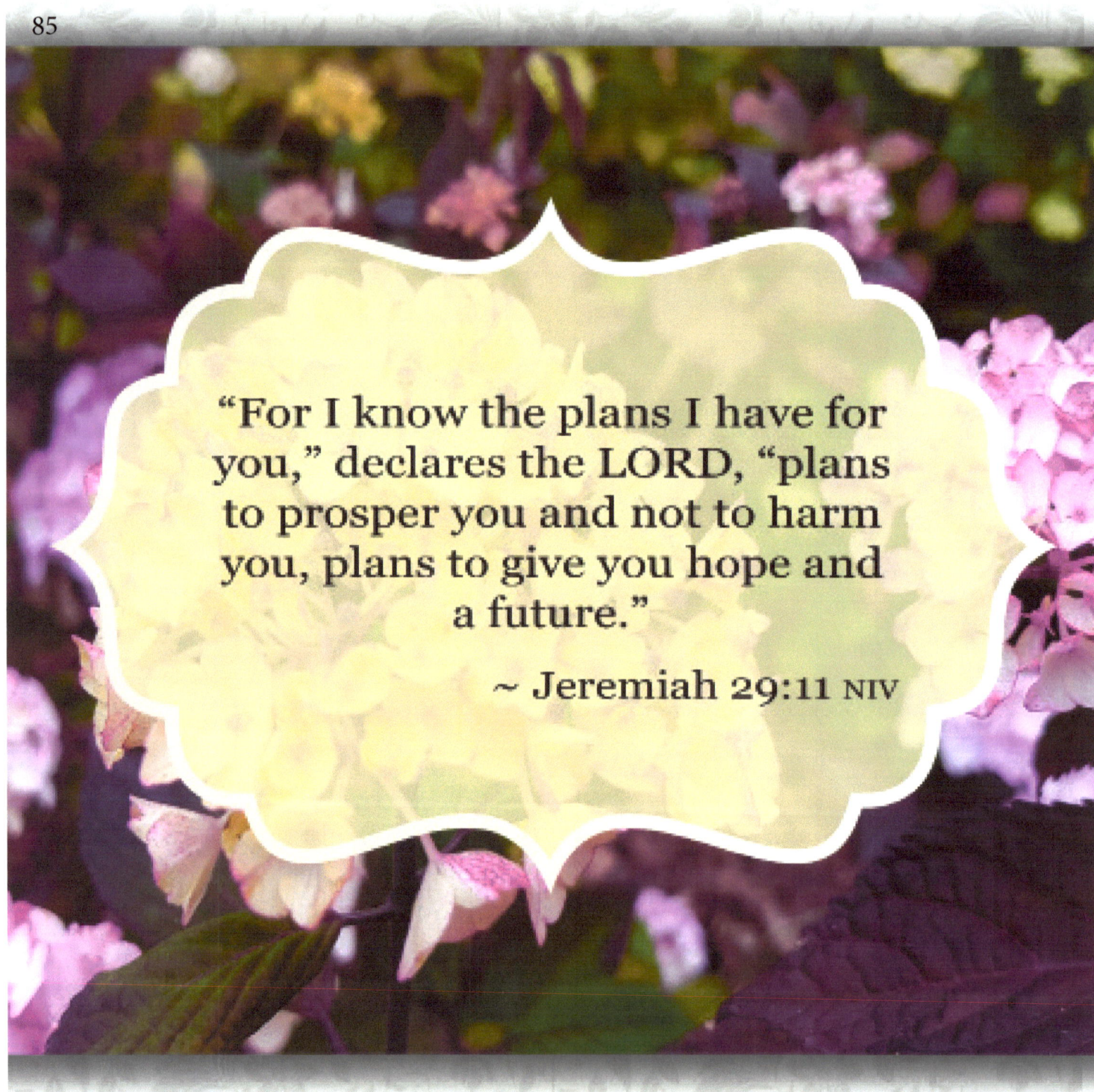

"For I know the plans I have for you," declares the LORD, "plans to prosper you and not to harm you, plans to give you hope and a future."

~ Jeremiah 29:11 NIV

Inspired Living Tip

Our lives are a gift to those
we are connected to.
Cherish these sweet blessings.

~ Anita Sechesky

"Be joyful in hope, patient in affliction, faithful in prayer."

~ Romans 12:12 NIV

I don't know what you're going through, but I know that you are loved.

~ Anita Sechesky

It's okay to let yourself cry. Tears release toxins which shift your internal energy to create room for healing.

~Anita Sechesky

About The Author

Anita Sechesky RN, ICF-CPC
#1 Best-Selling Author, Founder, CEO and Publisher at LWL PUBLISHING HOUSE

Anita is a wife and the mother of two boys, ages 17 & 11, the author & Visionary of multiple Best-Selling books in the Inspirational Self-Healing genre, and a Motivational Keynote Speaker.

Anita has successfully published over 100 Best-Selling authors. She enjoys hosting *Inspired to Write* workshops, Masterclasses on Emotional Healing, and speaking at events that focus on living your best life possible without emotional limitations.

Anita has worked in many health care facilities and Emergency Rooms in Southwestern Ontario and has witnessed the fragility that one's deterioration of health and well-being can impact the human spirit and family dynamics. It is her greatest desire that she can promote healing of not only the body, but also the mind and spirit of each man, woman and child through her vision.

If you would like to have Anita speak at your event or organization, or if you are interested in writing your own inspired story and would like to work with Anita to help you bring your best efforts forward to publication, please contact her below. Lastly, if you are interested in joining one of her Masterclasses on Emotional Healing, please visit our website and subscribe to our mailing list to stay updated on future events.

Website: www.lwlpublishinghouse.com
Email: lwlclienthelp@gmail.com